Young ones of animals require thoughtful care. That is why when there are lambs, calves, kids, piglets, or chicks on the farm, farmers are much busier.

Grooming horses needs special skills...

...just like caring for beehives.

Stables, sties, and cages need cleaning. The manure must be raked up, collected with a pitchfork or shovel, put into wheelbarrows, and placed in manure heaps. Manure is valuable for the soil, so it is spread once or twice a year and ploughed into the fields.

Whenever possible, the animals are driven out to pastures outside the village.

Then at sunset, they are driven back to their stables and stalls.

DOMESTIC CHICKENS

They are the early rising, scratching members of the farmyard.

hen / egglayer

cockerel / cock

A teenage chicken (from 8-10 weeks of age) is either called a pullet (female) or a cockerel (male).

The laying hen lays eggs, which the farmer collects on a daily basis. A chick is only born from an egg if there is a cockerel around the house. The eggs are incubated by the hen for 21 days before the chicks hatch.

Did you know?

Chickens do not sweat. They pant to protect themselves from the heat or, simply, bathe in the dust.

What do chickens eat?

seeds

insects

worms

snails

greens

corn

Chickens cluck, which sounds like 'bock-bock', peck, and scratch in the poultry yard all day long. After sunset, the farmer puts them in the chicken coop so that dogs, cats, foxes and other predators cannot steal them.

The Cockerel...

- its body is covered with colourful, ornate plumage,
- it signals the sunrise by crowing,
- it attracts hens by dancing when mating,
- it can be very aggressive.

Hens can even fight over who sits higher in the coop.

DOMESTIC DUCKS

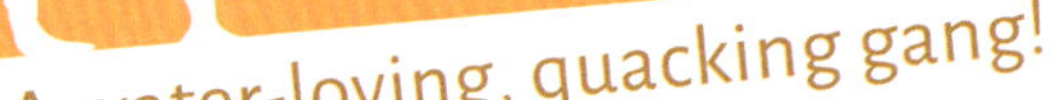
A water-loving, quacking gang!

drake

The drake may hurt the hens and ducklings, if kept together, in the same yard.

The hen lays eggs. If there is a drake around the house, fluffy little yellow-brown ducklings hatch 28 days later. The ducklings leave the nest immediately and waddle off after their mother.

hen

duckling

snow-white plumage	boat-shaped body	webbed feet	elongated head	flat, yellow bill
		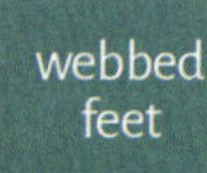 	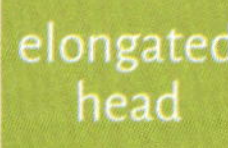	 

The ancestor of domesticated ducks is the mallard.

What do ducks feed on?

wheat

corn

seeds

insects

greens

aquatic plants

Ducks are fantastic swimmers!

About ducks...

What makes ducks fantastic swimmers?

The shape of their body, their webbed feet and their feathers, which are made waterproof by rubbing them with oil from the preen gland near their tails.

Why don't ducks feel the cold in water?

Because there's air trapped between their feathers and under their skin a thick layer of fat can be found.

Why do ducks have wide lamellate bills?

This type of bill enables them to filter the food from water, sand or mud.

Did you know?

Ducks are cheeky! They often get their eggs hatched by domestic hens.

?!!

Is your pillow filled with duck feathers?

DOMESTIC GEESE

Geese are honking farmyard fowls.

The goose lays less frequently than the hen. Depending on the breed it lays 30-50 eggs a year. Hatching youngs are called goslings (and baby geese only up to the age of two days).

gander

Ganders give a hissing sound when a stranger enters their territory.

goose

gosling

What do geese feed on?

grasses

grains

greens

Its ancestor is the wild grey leg goose.

Another name for a goose can be a fowl.

What are geese bred for?

meat

roasting

feather

liver

Fun fact

People sometimes say 'silly goose', although geese are incredibly intelligent. They are excellent watchdogs; they will call out loudly when an intruder enters. They're so vigilant that they used to be kept to protect castles from night-time poachers.

Did you know?

Saint Martin hid in a goose pen when trying to avoid being ordained bishop, but the cackling of the geese gave him away.

The term used for a group of geese is flock.

DOMESTIC PIGEONS

Navigational experts who live in the dovecotes.

hen

cock

squab

Did you know?

The pigeon selects its food based on what it sees; it prefers round or oval seeds with smooth surfaces.

The hen lays one or two eggs a few times a year. A peculiarity of pigeons is that hens produce 'milk' in their crop to feed their squabs for the first few days. The squabs leave the nest at 4-5 weeks of age.

Its ancestor is the Rock Dove (Columbia Livia).

What do pigeons feed on?

corn

sunflower

canary grass

wheat

soybean

peas

flaxseed

common millet

young shoot

SOME FACTS

- Pigeons can find their way home from very far away because they can navigate using the earth's magnetic field.
- In the past, carrier pigeons used to deliver messages.
- There are pigeon races for specially trained homing carrier pigeons today.
- Cocks court hens beautifully. That is why we call human lovers 'lovebirds'.
- The dove is considered a messenger of peace, a symbol of harmony and the soul.

DOMESTIC RABBITS

buck

A doe can produce 3-6 young ones a few times a year. The newborn rabbits are called kittens or kits.

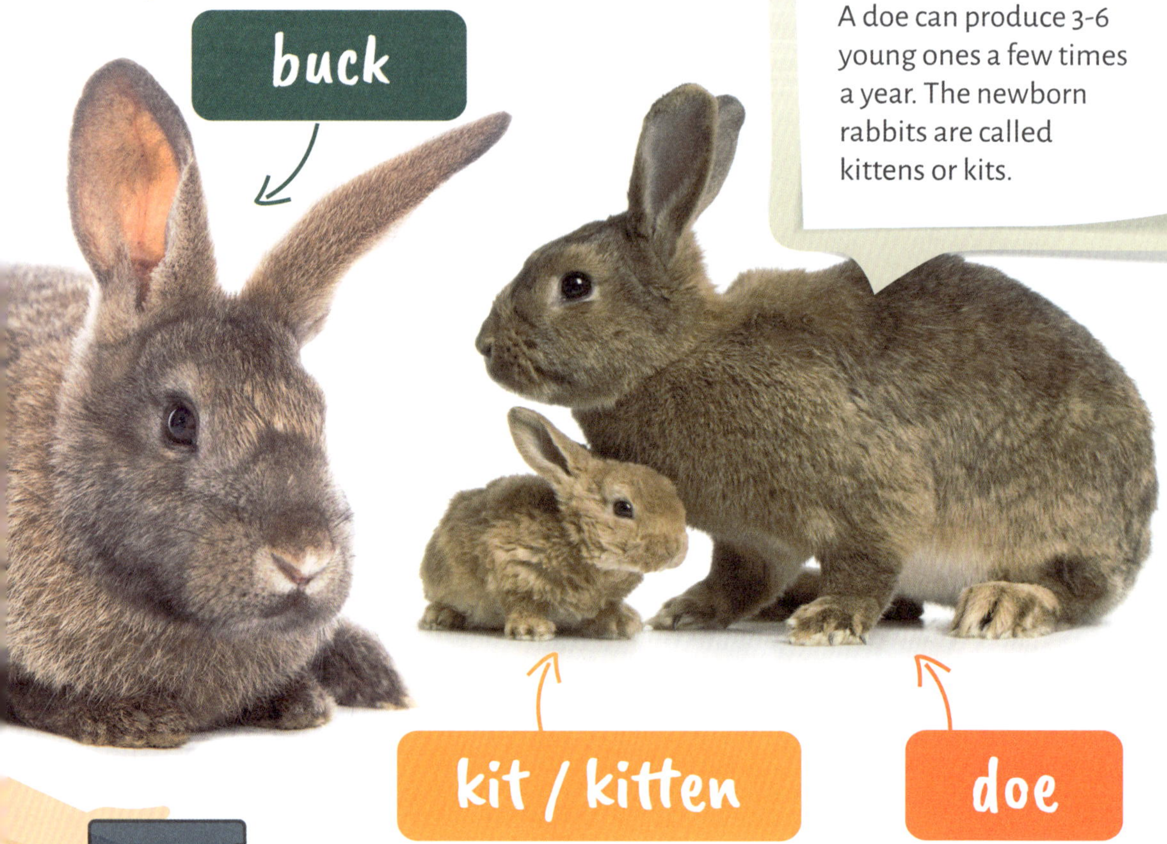

kit / kitten

doe

Did you know?

- Rabbits use their ears to help regulate their body temperature.
- They constantly wiggle their nose not just for smelling, but also for communication.
- Rabbits are sociable; they like company.
- They like to run around, zigzagging in the open, making them harder to catch.

Fun fact

Chewing helps wear down the rabbit's constantly growing top front teeth (incisors).

The European rabbit is considered the ancestor of the domestic rabbit.

What do rabbits eat?

grasses

chickweed

dandelion

clover

greens

shoots

hay

The rabbit is lying flat to the ground with its ears flattened against its back. *It is frightened.*

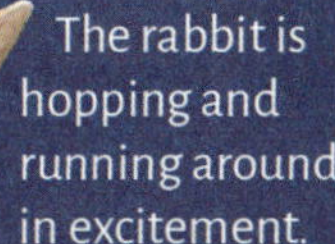

The rabbit is hopping and running around in excitement. *It is happy.*

The rabbit is lying down with an extended body. *It feels good.*

The rabbit is thumping on the ground with its hind legs. *It senses danger, or it is angry or scared.*

Do you know what it means when a rabbit does this?

DOMESTIC PIGS

Curly-tailed ones who love wallowing.

boar

saw

Twice a year, the sow farrows 5-12 piglets at a time, which she nurses for 5-7 weeks. During this period, the young are called suckling piglets, piglet from weaning, and gilts from the age of four months.

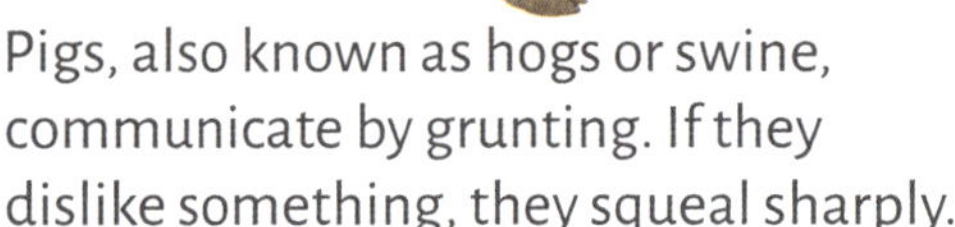

Pigs, also known as hogs or swine, communicate by grunting. If they dislike something, they squeal sharply.

A good nap after lunch.

A group of pigs is called a drift or a drove.

A wild boar

The domestic pig originates from the Eurasian wild boar.

What do pigs feed on?

Pigs are omnivores.

It has been proven by numerous studies that pigs...

- are intelligent,
- are emotional,
- learn quickly,
- show self-awareness!

Did you know?

Some religions prohibit the consumption of pork.

Why are pigs farmed?

DOMESTIC CATTLE

The patchy colourful lowing herd.

bull

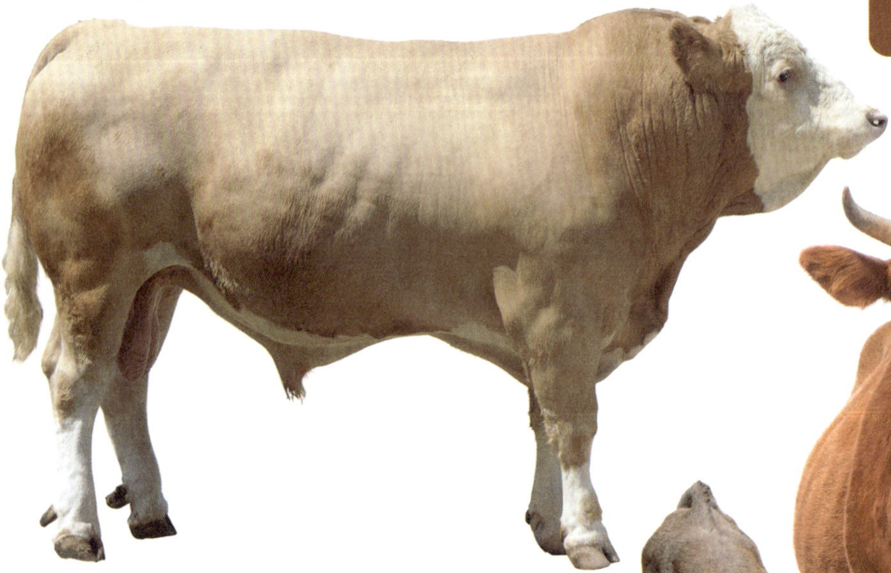

cow

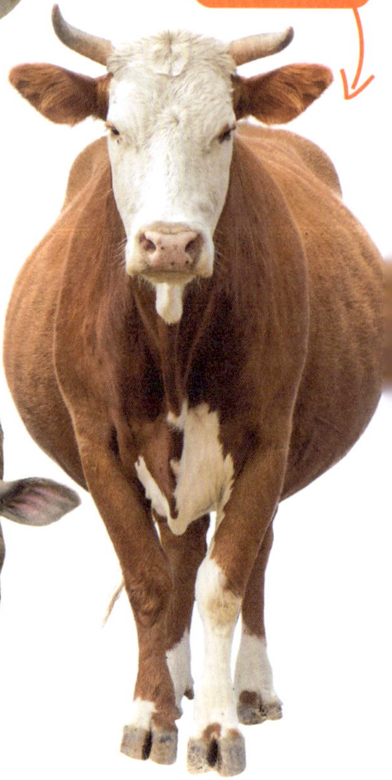

Once a year, cows give birth to one calf. Calves can come in different colours depending on the breed, but they are usually reddish-orange or black and white.

calf

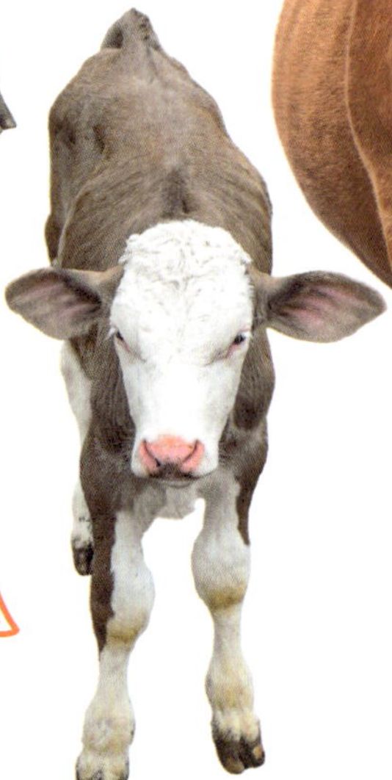

What do cattle feed on?

herbaceous plants

grasses

feed

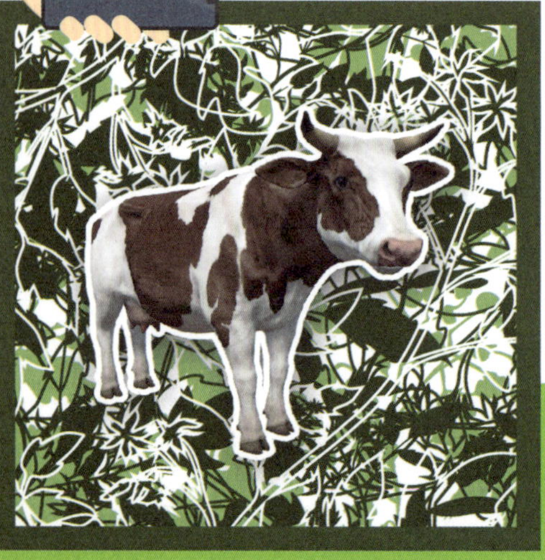

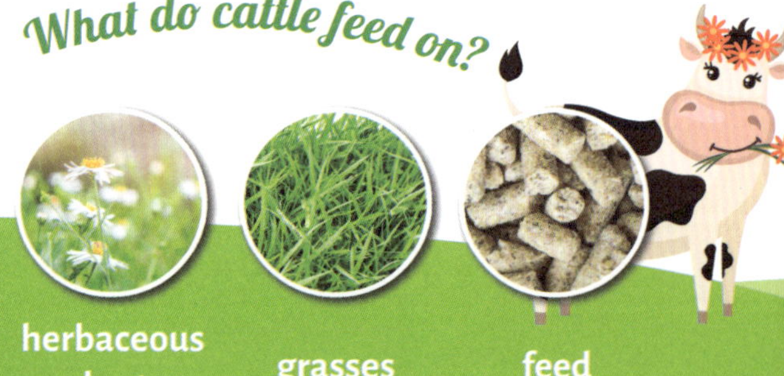

Fun fact

Cattle are considered sacred in India. Some religions of the world strictly prohibit the slaughter of cows.

The more you study, the more you know.

About cattle...

herd – a group of cattle grazing in the pasture
drove – a group of cattle kept outdoors from spring to autumn
heifer – a female calf
steer – a castrated young bull
ox – a castrated adult male

In the old days, oxen used to be put in front of the cart or plough.

Did you know?

When cows eat, the food travels to the rumen, from which it is later coughed up, and chewed again. This is called **rumination**.

What are cattle raised for?

dairy products

meat

The ancestor of the cattle is the wild ox of Europe.

DOMESTIC SHEEP

A bleating flock of sheep with very good memories.

For sheep, the male and female are similar in size. The ram has curling horns. Once a year, the ewe usually produces twins.

ewe

Lambs are fed on milk until they are 2-3 months old. When called by its mother, the lamb rushes to her wagging its tail. If the lamb leaves its mother, it cries with a long, long bleat.

lamb

Sheep are social creatures. They feel safe in the flock. Sheep even make friends with each other.

What do sheep eat?
grasses
plants
feed
What are sheep raised for?
dairy products
meat
wool
Sheep meat is called mutton.
Sheep shearing
The thick coat of sheep is sheared in spring or early summer to produce wool.
Most likely, its ancestor is the wild mouflon.
a group of sheep = a flock

DOMESTIC GOATS

Climbing champions with wobbly voices.

doe

buck

kid

In general, both does and bucks have horns and a beard.

In spring, the mother goat produces 1-3 kids at a time. The kids quickly become independent. They start growing their horns as early as two months old. The horns are fully developed by the age of one year.

Did you know?

Goats are not demanding animals. They don't mind living in sparsely vegetated or even barren areas.

What do goats feed on?

grasses

fodder beet

hay

weeds

vegetables

fruits

The goat used to be called 'poor man's cow'.

It is curious and playful.

It is from goats that the ancient Greeks learned how to prune grapes, which made them worship these animals as saints.

Why are goats farmed?

a group of goats = a flock

Goats in Morocco often graze in trees. They love eating Argan fruit!

DOMESTIC HORSES

Horses are magnificent hoofed creatures in studs.

foal

mare

stallion

Galloping is a necessity for horses by nature.

A mare usually has a foal once a year. The foal is running and jumping around alone for the first few days, but later it prefers playing with its buddies.

Did you know?

Horse fodder may contain, for example, oats, barley, corn, and wheat.

oats

barley

wheat

corn

a group of horses = a stable / herd

I am coming, Princess!

The ancestor of the domestic horse is the wild horse.

What do horses eat?

grasses

alfalfa

hay

cereals (fodder)

oilseeds, legumes

carrots, fodder beet, sugar beet

apples

pumpkin

Do you know what it means when a horse does this?

It is nickering.
It says hello to you.

It raises its tail high.
It wants to play.

It throws its head over another horse.
It's a sign of trust or love.

It is neighing.
It's looking for its mate.

Its ears are pointing to the sky.
It is watchful.

Its tail is dangling down.
It is tired and sleepy.

DOMESTIC DONKEYS

Reliable load carriers.

jenny / mane

jack

A jenny usually gives birth to one foal. The little donkey follows its caring mother everywhere.

foal

The donkey is a peaceful and calm animal. It is often called stubborn because when it senses danger, or is carrying a load that is too heavy, it stands in the same spot refusing to move.

What do donkeys eat?

The ancestor of the donkey is the African wild ass.

What are donkeys raised for?

carrying loads

milk

meat

FUN FACTS

- A mule is produced by the hybridisation between a jack (a male donkey) and a mare (a female horse).
- The life expectancy of a donkey can be as high as 50 years.
- Miniature donkeys exist, too.
- Rumour says Cleopatra, queen of Egypt, regularly bathed in donkey milk to preserve the beauty of her skin.
- In the past, donkey milk would play an important role as medicine.

Did you know?

The donkey is a good 'weatherman'. If it's going to rain, it starts braying.

DOMESTIC DOGS

Faithful guardians of livestock and the house.

The gestation period for dogs lasts for two months. Usually, 2-10 offspring are born. Newborn puppies sleep all day and feed on mother's milk.

dog

The puppies chew on everything, and they love playing and fighting with each other.

bitch

pup(py)

What do dogs eat?

meat | pet / dog food | dairy products

Did you know?

Dogs are digitigrade animals - meaning they walk with only their toes touching the ground.

Dogs are predators.

About dogs...

- Herding dogs control and protect the flock and herd.
- They are obedient, intelligent and loyal.
- Dogs are man's trusted companions.
- Dogs have a strong protective instinct.
- They bark loudly to signal an intruder.

The ancestor of the dog is the wolf.

Do you know what it means when a dog does this?

It pins its ears back.

It is afraid or ashamed.

Bright eyes.

It is waiting for an order.

It looks at you with its head tilted to one side.

It is interested.

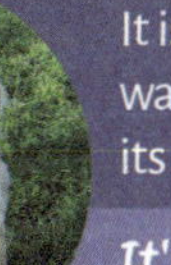

It is wagging its tail.

It's happy.

It bows and wags its tail.

It is inviting you to play.

It is growling, snarling and raises its hair. *It is aggressive.*

DOMESTIC CATS

Flattering carnivores.

tom

queen

kitten / kitty

The mother cat has 3-4 kittens at a time. The kittens are born with their eyes closed, and they do not open until 7-14 days. Initially, their vision is blurred.

The ancestor of the domestic cat is the Nubian cat.

What do cats eat?

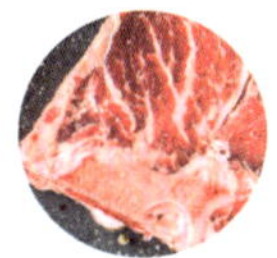

meat

dairy products

pet / cat food

Did you know?

- Cats are dangerous predators!
- It catches rodents around the house, protecting our pantry.
- A cat stalks its prey by stealth, but only eats it when it's starving.
- For a cat, it's all about the thrill of the hunt.

The cat is purring.

The cat feels good.

Its fur stands on end.

It is frightened.

It is rubbing against your leg.

It is hungry.

The kitty is meowing.

It is asking for food or inviting you to play.

The cat is wagging its tail.

It is excited.

Do you know what it means when your cat does this?

DOMESTIC BEES

Buzzing swarm of honey bees.

eggs

The eggs are the future offspring.

drone

There are a few hundred males, called drones, whose job is to mate.

Did you know?

The drones and workers that hatch in the spring live for only about 50 days, while the ones that hatch in autumn survive the winter and live until the following spring. The lifespan of a queen bee is 4-5 years.

The mother bee, also known as the queen, mates with many drones in her life. She lays her eggs continuously - up to 1500 a day - into the beeswax honeycomb built by the drones. From the eggs, a queen bee, workers or drones are hatched. The queen bee is the only fertile female of the honeybee family.

worker

The work is done by several tens of thousands of workers.

queen bee

Worker bees are infertile females.

Honey bees are related to wasps and ants.

What do bees feed on?

The domestic bee is also known as the honey bee.

Bee houses around our homes

hive / beehive

Bees...

- live in families,
- communicate with each other,
- can fly several kilometres to collect the nectar for honey,
- make honey and royal jelly,
- huddle together in clusters in the cold.

The tasks of worker bees include

- building the honeycomb
- raising offspring
- feeding the queen-to-be with royal jelly
- gathering pollen, nectar, water and propolis

The functions of drones include

- lazing around
- mating

The queen bee is responsible for

- providing the offspring

TABLE OF CONTENTS

List of 3D models